OUR WILDLIFE WORLD

PANDAS

Merebeth Switzer

Grolier

TORONTO

FACTS IN BRIEF

Classification of the Giant Panda
Class: *Mammalia* (mammals)
Order: *Carnivora* (carnivores)
Family: *Procyonidae** (raccoon family)
Genus: *Ailuropoda*
Species: *Ailuropoda melanoleuca*

* Many scientists disagree, but at present this is still the classification usually given.

Distribution.   Central China near Tibet border.

Distinctive physical characteristics.   Striking black and white markings; bear-like shape; extra digit on forepaws used like a thumb.

Habitat.   Bamboo forests at altitudes of 2000–3500 metres (6500–11 500 feet).

Habits.   Solitary; establishes territory by scent markings; active day and night, alternating periods of feeding and resting.

Diet.   Chiefly bamboo. Other vegetable matter and meat make up less than 1 percent of the panda's diet.

Canadian Cataloguing in Publication Data

Switzer, Merebeth.
  Pandas

(Our wildlife world ; 1)
ISBN 0-7172-2255-1

1. Pandas—Juvenile literature.
I. Title. II. Series.

QL737.C214S85 1987   j599.74'443   C87-095243-9

Contents

What is black and white and loved all over? The Giant Panda, of course! Each year, millions of people travel to see these extraordinary animals at the few zoos where they are on display.

Why are we "panda crazy?" Perhaps because the round furry pandas look so cuddly and are so amusing to watch as they lumber lazily around or playfully turn somersaults. Sometimes they'll even stop in the middle of the roll and hold the position for a while.

But pandas are not simply cute. They are amazing animals and until recently their life was full of secrets. Join us now as we unravel the mystery of one of the world's most popular animals.

In a Quiet Forest

In a dense bamboo forest a panda sits, leaning back against a tree surrounded by the dark green of the forest. She has something cradled in her arm, something that she is gently stroking with her large paw. Why, it's a baby panda!

The panda cub is about ten weeks old. It was tiny, naked and completely helpless at birth, but it is growing quickly and already has a coat of fine white and black fur. Its eyes have opened, and soon it will be ready to take its first unsteady steps.

For now, however, the baby panda is content to snuggle against its mother's warm body and peacefully nurse on her rich milk. The cub has a lot more growing to do, and its mother will be very busy caring for it during the months to come.

A Bamboo Forest Home

Pandas live in central China near the border of Tibet. They make their home in bamboo forests high in the mountains where it is always very cool. Even in summer the temperature seldom rises above that of a nice spring day, about 15°C (60°F).

Not only is this dense wilderness cool, it is also very rainy and shrouded in cloud and fog for most of the year. Snow falls from late November to early April.

The panda is not completely alone in the forest, nor is bamboo the only thing that grows there. Deer, golden marmoset, monkeys and Lesser Pandas pad through the bamboo. And hardy evergreen trees, such as dragon spruce, spider pine, fir and hemlock, also thrive in this cool, damp climate.

Although some pandas can be found lower down or higher up, most make their homes at altitudes of 2000–3000 metres (7000–10 000 feet).

Animal of Mystery

The Giant Panda has always been very rare. And its lonely forest home and secret ways mean that few people have known the panda firsthand. Chinese farmers that live near the panda have stories dating back centuries. They call the panda *beishung,* a word that means "white bear."

The panda was a mystery to the western world until the 1920s. The first live panda was brought to North America in 1936, and even today only a few zoos outside China are home to the Giant Pandas.

Perhaps one of the most mysterious things about the Giant Panda is its name, because it isn't really a giant at all. It is only about one metre (3 feet) tall from the ground to the top of its back. And it would take more than 30 of these "giants" to tip the scale with an elephant.

Pandas love water and may drink
until their tummies bloat.

Opposite page:
The Lesser Panda looks more like a raccoon or a cat than it does like its famous black and white relative.

The Lesser Panda

Perhaps the explanation of the Giant Panda's name lies in the existence of a much more common but much smaller relative, the Lesser Panda. Also known as the Red Panda because of its soft, thick, chestnut-colored coat, the Lesser Panda too lives in the bamboo forests of the Himalayan Mountains. Its range, however, is not nearly as restricted as that of the Giant Panda.

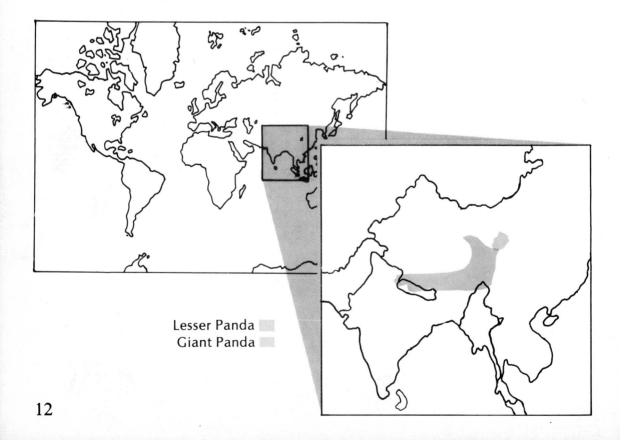

Lesser Panda
Giant Panda

Figuring Out the Family

Although scientists have recently spent a great deal of time learning about the Giant Panda, they still disagree about the panda's family tree.

To understand the problem, we need to look more closely at the Red Panda. The Red Panda looks like a red raccoon. It even has a raccoon-like mask and rings on its bushy tail. Some scientists think these pandas are very close cousins to the Giant Panda and classify both as members of the raccoon family.

Many other scientists, however, looking at the Giant Panda's bear-like features, believe that this panda is more closely related to bears. Finally a third group of scientists think that the Red and the Giant Pandas deserve to be placed in their own special ''panda'' group.

Yum . . . It certainly looks as though the panda's sense of taste is better than its eyesight. Pandas also hear well and have an acute sense of smell.

Black and White and Warm All Over

When you are looking at pictures of animals, you may have trouble knowing for sure whether you are seeing an elk or a cariboo, a cheetah or a leopard. But you always know a panda when you see one.

People often wonder whether any purpose is served by the distinctive black and white pattern of the panda's fur. No one can know for sure, but one theory is that it helps pandas keep out of each other's way. Pandas are loners and definitely prefer to meet as little as possible. Their eyesight, however, is rather poor. It is thought that their sharply contrasting coloration may make it easier for them to spot one another in time to avoid unwelcome encounters.

Whatever the reason for its color scheme, the panda's coat is wonderfully suited to its cool, damp mountain home. Thick and oily, it keeps the panda warm and dry through all kinds of weather.

Bamboo for Breakfast, Lunch and Dinner

Over 99% of the panda's diet is bamboo. But because bamboo is 90% water, it is not very nourishing. What's more, the panda's digestive system is not very efficient. This means that the panda must spend a lot of time eating. And it does. In fact, a panda spends anywhere from 10 to 16 hours every day feasting on 10 to 15 kilograms (20 to 30 pounds) of this tough plant!

What is this food that pandas find so tasty? Bamboo is a type of giant woody grass that can grow to be taller than most people and even as big as some small trees. Bamboo is very tough and strong. In fact, its dried stalks are used to make furniture. Perhaps you have sat in a bamboo chair yourself.

The rough, straight stalks of bamboo have ring-like bumps all along their length. Branches grow from these bumps and leaves sprout along the branches. The panda prefers the bamboo leaves, but it also eats the stem, sometimes pulling off pieces of outer fibrous "bark" to snack on the tender insides.

Opposite page:
Pandas usually sit upright while feeding.

19

Sometimes Snacks

People say that "variety is the spice of life." A panda might agree, but would add that a little spice goes a long, long way.

Sometimes, when it is wanting a treat or when food is scarce, a panda will munch on vines, grasses and even wild roots such as parsnips. Occasionally it will eat meat as well. (In fact, for various reasons, scientists classify pandas in the order of carnivores, that is, meat-eaters.) But since it is not a good hunter it must make do with the leftovers of a leopard's hunting trip. The panda also has a sweet tooth and a reputation for robbing village beehives for a sweet treat of honey.

Still, these various sources of food won't fill up a panda and it cannot live on these alone. Without bamboo the panda cannot survive.

For a panda, anytime is mealtime.

Hard Times

The bamboo forests where pandas live are dotted throughout central China. Each forest has at least one type of bamboo growing in it, and in some there are three or four. Pandas eat whatever types of bamboo grow in their particular forest, and as we have seen, they eat very little else. This occasionally creates a serious problem for the panda.

Bamboo plants grow by sending up new green shoots from their roots each spring. This means that every year millions of new stems are produced. But after some years—it may be 15 or it may be 100, depending on the type—the bamboo stops growing. Instead, it sprouts flowers which form seeds and then the whole plant dies. The seeds fall to the ground and begin the long process of developing into new plants. It takes at least two years for new bamboo plants to grow. So if only one kind of bamboo grows in that particular forest, the pandas living there are without their most important food for a very long time.

*Opposite page:
While they spend most of their time on the ground, pandas sometimes climb trees for shelter or refuge.*

*The next time you
eat Chinese food
think of this: the
crunchy vegetable
you are enjoying
may be the same
bamboo that
pandas love.*

Thumb

*Panda's front
paw.*

The Panda's Thumb

Try spending the entire day without using your
thumb. You'll be surprised at how important it
is to have one. Without a thumb, it's very
difficult to write a letter, peel an orange, pick up
a penny or even steer a bike. A panda doesn't
need to do any of these things, but it does need
its thumb to eat. In fact, without this marvelous
tool, the panda might starve.

To understand why the panda's thumb is so
special let's look at how it works. On each of its
front paws, a panda has five fingers *plus* a
thumb—which is really one of its wrist bones.
You can feel this bone in your own wrist: it is the
large bump where your arm and hand meet.

In a panda, this bone has become very long
with extra nerves and muscles that help it to
work properly. Once the panda's five fingers
have grabbed a stalk of bamboo, it jams it up
against its thumb-like wrist bone. With the
bamboo "locked" into its paw, the panda can
begin to eat without fear of dropping its meal.

Crunching a Tough Meal

Bamboo is a tough plant, but the panda is well equipped to eat it. The panda's powerful jaws cut off a broom-handle-thick stalk of bamboo in one mighty crunch. Then the panda sits back on its haunches, strips off the parts it does not want to eat, and begins to munch. It takes only seconds for the panda's big flat teeth to grind up and crush an entire bamboo stalk. Then it's on to the next . . .

Bamboo splinters are very sharp but the panda is well protected against their piercing points. The inside walls of the panda's esophagus—the tube leading from its mouth to its stomach—are extra strong and resist damage from the needle-sharp bamboo.

A panda can chew through bamboo stems 4 centimetres (1.5 inches) thick.

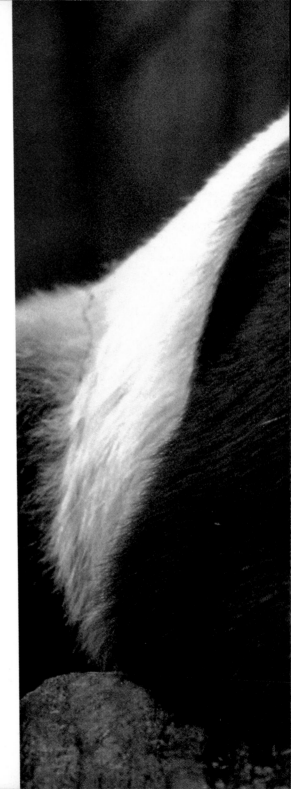

Snacking and Snoozing

Pandas don't keep regular hours,
nor do they have a regular resting
place. They spend much of their
time both day and night munching
their way around their territory.
When they feel tired, they simply
flop themselves down for a snooze
wherever they happen to be.

If the weather is very bad a panda
may seek out the shelter of a cave or
a hollow old tree stump. But most
of the time it is perfectly happy
sleeping in the open—especially in
the middle of a stand of bamboo.
That way it doesn't have to move if
it wants a mid-snooze snack.

Nap time.

Rambling and Rolling

If you have ever seen a panda walking with its pigeon-toed, rolling gait, you will know that it doesn't move very quickly. A panda spends most of its life within its "home range"—an area that is about two to three kilometres (1 to 2 miles) in diameter. But because it stops so frequently to sit and eat, a panda usually only covers an area about the size of a football field each day.

Sometimes a panda may roam farther afield if food is scarce or if it is in search of a mate.

Pandas are seldom in a hurry.

Panda Signposts

Pandas live alone in their bamboo forest and they prefer it that way. However they do have several ways to leave messages for other pandas. Like some forest animals, such as the bear or the lynx, pandas rake their claws on the trunks of trees. This scrapes off large sections of bark and leaves the message "Panda at home."

Pandas also leave "scent" messages. Each panda has glands near the base of its stubby little tail. These glands contain a strong smelling "panda perfume." By rubbing its bottom against a rock or piece of ground, the panda lets other pandas know it's been around.

Pandas are usually quiet but when they meet one another they are very noisy. They make bear-like grunts and moans, and bleating sounds a bit like a cross between the *moo* of a cow and the *baa* of a sheep. Baby pandas call for their mother's attention with a loud, high-pitched squawk.

Opposite page:
Although pandas look cute and cuddly, they can defend themselves very well when threatened.

Finding a Mate

When spring arrives, a male panda sets out to seek a mate. Pandas usually find each other by calling, but the male is also helped in its search by any claw rakings or scent markings the female panda may have recently made. If two males come upon a female at the same time, they will often have mock battles and "roaring contests." These last until one, generally the weaker, gives up and goes away.

Whether she has several suitors or just one, the female will usually play hard-to-get for a time. If the male is over-eager and comes too close before she has got used to him, she may slap or even bite him and take refuge up a tree. He might then have to wait several days for her to relent and accept his attentions.

Unless food is scarce, a panda will seldom leave its home range except in search of a mate.

A Cub is Born

The male panda leaves after mating. Three to five months later, the mother panda prepares a den in a rock cave or at the base of a tree. Here her tiny pink cub will be born, weighing not much more than a small apple.

The panda is a devoted mother. For the first few weeks of her cub's life she carries it wherever she goes, cradling it against her body to keep it warm. Once it is a bit bigger and its fur has grown in, she may carry it by its neck like a mother cat with her kitten. Now she sometimes tucks the cub safely into the hollow of a tree while she feeds nearby.

A panda is a loving mother and fiercely protective of her tiny cub.

Growing Up

The panda cub grows quickly but remains quite helpless for the first two months of its life. When it is three or four months old it starts to crawl. By the time it is seven months old it can run, climb trees and even eat bamboo.

Although a baby panda has no brothers or sisters to play with, it seems to be able to amuse itself anywhere. One panda was even seen sliding down a hill on its tummy and climbing back up to do it again. And like most mothers, the mother panda takes part in her baby's games and is always ready for a bit of roughhousing.

The mother keeps a close eye on her growing youngster. An adult panda has very few natural enemies but the small cub can fall prey to leopards or Asiatic wild dogs.

This panda cub has grown enormously since it was born four or five months ago. By the time it is a year old it will weigh about 25–35 kilograms (55–80 pounds), or more than 200 times what it did at birth.

Leaving Home

By the time the cub is nine months old it no longer needs its mother's milk. Nonetheless, it stays with her a bit longer.

Finally, however, even though it is not fully grown and still has a lot of weight to put on, the time comes for the young panda to leave and find its own territory. Young male pandas will wander quite far but young female pandas tend to stay closer to the mother's territory. In another four to six years, the young panda will be ready to start a family of its own.

Taking it easy.

Finding Out About Pandas

Because there are so few pandas in the world, the Chinese government has declared them a "national treasure" and established special reserves for them to live in safely. Recently scientists have spent time in these reserves to learn more about pandas.

Pandas live alone in very dense forests and are not easy to learn about. Researchers look for clawed tree trunks, fresh paw prints or trampled grass where a panda may have slept. Once they find a panda they trap it and give it a sedative so it falls asleep. They make sure it is healthy, weigh it and put a small radio collar around its neck.

By the time the panda wakes up it is free to wander away again, but the researchers can keep track of where it goes. This helps them to learn more about the size of the panda's territory and its daily movements.

The more we learn about pandas, the less likely we are to carelessly do them harm and the more we can help any that find themselves in trouble.

Words to Know

Bamboo   A giant tropical grass with woody, hollow stems and hard, thick joints from which branches sprout.

Carnivore   Literally, "meat-eater." Scientists classify animals as belonging to the order *Carnivora* (carnivores) on the basis of various physical characteristics. Pandas have these characteristics and are therefore classified as carnivores even though they very rarely eat meat.

Den   Animal home.

Diameter   A straight line passing through the center of a circle from one side to the other.

Esophagus   The tube through which food passes from the mouth to the stomach.

Gland   A part of an animal's body that makes and gives out a substance.

Home range   The area that an animal regularly travels.

Mate   To come together to produce young. Either member of an animal pair is also the other's mate.

Order   A grouping used in classifying animals and plants. An order is smaller than a *class* and larger than a *family*.

Territory   Area that an animal (or a group of animals) lives in and often defends from other animals of the same kind. An animal may have a *home range* much larger than its *territory*.

INDEX

Cover Photo: Zig Leszczynski (Animals, Animals)

Photo Credits: Robert C. Simpson (Valan Photos), pages 4, 18, 45; Mark Sherman (Bruce Coleman Inc.), page 9; Peter Richardson (The Stock Market, Inc.), page 10; Bill Ivy, page 13; D. De Mello (New York Zoological Society), pages 14, 42; Bill Meng (New York Zoological Society), pages 17, 31, 32; Norman Myers (Bruce Coleman Inc.), pages 20-21; Zig Leszczynski (Animals, Animals), pages 23, 28; Gordon J. Fisher (The Stock Market, Inc.), page 24; Y.R. Tymstra (Valan Photos), page 27; Metro Toronto Zoo, page 34; Greg Locke (The Stock Market, Inc.), page 37; Chris Elliott (World Wildlife Federation), page 38; Zhu Jing (World Wildlife Federation), page 41; George B. Schaller, page 46.

Illustration page 7: Marianne Collins